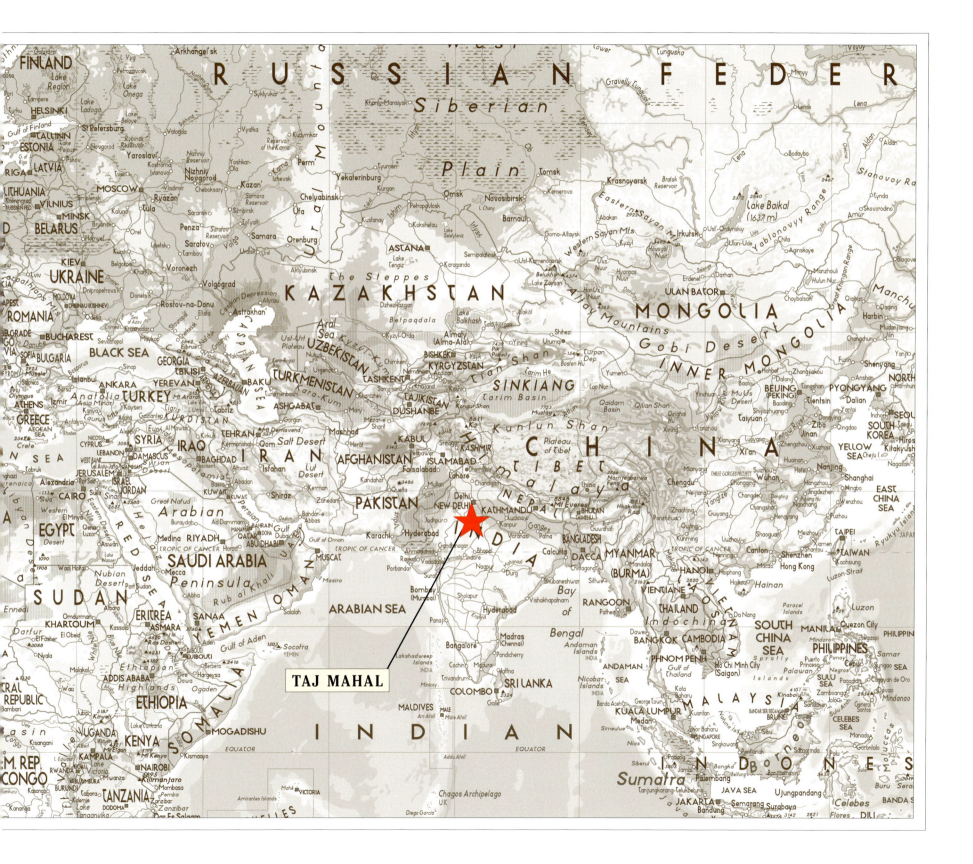

TAJ MAHAL

Published by Creative Education
123 South Broad Street
Mankato, Minnesota 56001

Creative Education is an imprint of The Creative Company.

Designed by Stephanie Blumenthal
Production design by The Design Lab
Art direction by Rita Marshall

Photographs by Corbis (Archivo Iconografico, S.A., David Ball, Tom Bean, Bettmann, Michael Boys, Elio Ciol, Ric Ergenbright, Robert Essel NYC, Freelance Consulting Services Pty Ltd, Peter Guttman, George Hall, Martin Harvey, Lindsay Hebberd, Chris Hellier, Jeremy Horner, Craig Lovell, Renee Lynn, Francis G. Mayer, Douglas Peebles, Richard Powers, Carl & Ann Purcell, Charles O'Rear, Diego Lezama Orezzoli, Reuters, David Samuel Robbins, Kevin Schafer, Stapleton Collection, Swim Ink, Roger Tidman, Brian A. Vikander, Nevada Wier, Jim Zuckerman), Getty Images (Taxi)

Printed in the United States of America

Library of Congress Cataloging-in-Publication Data
Shofner, Shawndra.
Taj Mahal / by Shawndra Shofner.
p. cm. — (Ancient wonders of the world)
Includes index.
ISBN 978-1-58341-361-6
1. Taj Mahal (Agra, India)—Juvenile literature. 2. Architecture, Mogul—India—Agra—Juvenile literature.
3. Agra (India)—Buildings, structures, etc.—Juvenile literature. I. Title. II. Series.

NA6183.S56 2005   726'.8'09542—dc22   2004056242

2 4 6 8 9 7 5 3

Taj Mahal

SHAWNDRA SHOFNER

CREATIVE EDUCATION

TAJ MAHAL

Like other ancient gardens, the Taj Mahal and its grounds reflect a desire for perfect symmetry. Despite its massive proportions, the elegant structure looks almost weightless.

Fifteen-year-old Arjumand Banu Begam waited on customers admiring her silks and glass beads when in swaggered 16-year-old Prince Khurram, the son of India's ruler. Smitten by her beauty, the prince asked the price of a diamond-shaped piece of glass. Arjumand flirted with him, saucily saying the diamond was real and that it cost more than he could afford. Speechless, Prince Khurram quickly shelled out her inflated price of 10,000 rupees, snatched the glass, and disappeared into the crowd. So began the real-life fairy tale between a future emperor and his queen, and the devotion he felt for her that is forever reflected in the world's most beautiful building: the Taj Mahal.

THE CHOSEN ONE

Mogul emperors delighted in watching convicted criminals writhe to their death from the bite of a poisonous snake taken from a basket kept near the throne. Another favorite torture of the time involved stitching a man into the wet skin of an animal and watching him suffocate as the drying skin shrank.

Akbar, Khurram's grandfather, had this miniature painting (right) made of himself on a tiger hunt.

From A.D. 1526 to 1707, a **lineage** of six **Mogul** emperors ruled what is now India. The first Mogul to conquer the throne was Khurram's great, great grandfather, Babar, whose ruthless ancestors included the Turkish conqueror Tamerlane and warrior Ghengis Kahn. Not surprisingly, bloody combat, gruesome tortures, and savage sports such as tiger hunting and watching elephant fights thrilled the Moguls.

Mogul rulers lived a frivolous, indulgent lifestyle. Their turbans flaunted emeralds and rubies, and their palace ceilings glimmered in pure gold. Musicians always played—even in empty rooms, just in case the emperor entered. Moguls devoted themselves to the **Muslim** religion of Islam, which allowed each man four wives. Most marriages were arrangements that sprang from political and military alliances, not personal choice or love. Literature, art, music, and drama carried religious themes, and the Moguls' death-wielding swords bore inscriptions from the **Koran**.

Royal astrologers chose March 27, 1612, as the date on which Prince Khurram—who already had one wife—married Arjumand. At their wedding feast, Emperor Jahangir honored his newest daughter-in-law with a new

6

Khurram was descended from a long line of powerful rulers, including Tamerlane, Babar, and Humayun (top), as well as the notorious Ghengis Kahn (pictured outside of his tent, bottom).

Whenever a Mogul emperor was crowned, he gave himself a new name that described the image he had of himself. Khurram gave himself the long and grand name "Abul Muzaffar Shihabuddin Mohammed Sahib Qiran-Sani Shah Jahan Badshah Ghazi," which was shortened to "Shah Jahan" for informal occasions.

name: Mumtaz Mahal, which means "Chosen One of the Palace." The wedding celebration lasted for an entire month, and from then on, the two were inseparable.

Unlike most **monarchies**, in which the king's first-born son is heir to the throne, Mogul emperors conquered the throne by a deadly process of elimination. When Emperor Jahangir died in late 1627, Prince Khurram vied for the empty throne by winning a battle in the city of Lahore (which is now the provincial capital of Punjab in northwest Pakistan) against his stepbrother, Shahriyar. Khurram immediate-

ly eliminated any other competition to the throne by killing his brothers, nephews, and male cousins. Khurram took the crown on February 4, 1628, and gave himself an extravagant new name, the shortened version of which is Shah Jahan: "The King of the World."

Shah Jahan spoiled Mumtaz Mahal with diamonds, fragrant roses, and majestic suites in the palace. Mumtaz traveled with Shah Jahan when he fought battles, living close by in tented war camps that were portable yet magnificent models of their permanent court. Every day, Shah Jahan consulted with Mumtaz on important matters of the empire.

In 1628, the Peacock Throne—lavished with emeralds, diamonds, pearls, sapphires, gold, and silver—was built to commemorate Shah Jahan's coronation. A little over a century later, Persian ruler Nadir Shah took the prized throne (then worth one million rupees, or about $21,600) after winning a battle over the Moguls in Delhi.

The rule of Shah Jahan (opposite) has been classified as the golden age of Mogul art and architecture and was characterized by beautifully ornamented pieces such as the Peacock Throne (left).

There are no existing portraits of Mumtaz Mahal, because *purdah*, the law of the veil, required Indian women to cover their faces in public or in the presence of men. Some artists sidestepped the law by sitting in one room and painting the mirrored reflections of a woman who sat unveiled in another room.

The white marble of the Taj Mahal creates the illusion that the monument is changing colors throughout the day, from blue to white to yellow.

The emperor placed so much faith in his wife's judgment that he trusted her with the *Muhr Uzak*, the emperor's seal of authority—a mark that even he could not reverse once stamped on a document.

In the couple's 19 years of marriage, they had 14 children, 7 of whom survived. While Shah Jahan directed a battle in 1630 against Khan Jahan Lodi, who controlled the Deccan Plateau in southern India, Mumtaz Mahal gave birth to their 14th child in a tent nearby. The emperor received news of a healthy baby girl but nothing of his wife's condition. After midnight, he received word that she was tired, resting comfortably, and wished to be alone.

Shah Jahan went to sleep, but he was soon awakened by an attendant with news that the queen needed him. He quickly joined her at her bedside, only to realize that the baby's delivery had been too difficult. By dawn, Mumtaz Mahal was dead.

Consumed with grief, Shah Jahan shut himself away for eight days. On the ninth day, he came out and ordered the entire empire into mourning for two years, prohibiting all music, feasting, and celebrations. In 1631, about 30 years before French King Louis XIV began building the magnificent palace at Versailles, Shah Jahan launched the construction of a monument that represented love like no other: the incredible Taj Mahal.

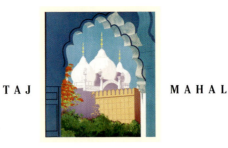

TAJ   MAHAL

TRIBUTE TO LOVE

Adhering to Mogul tradition, the coffin containing the remains of Mumtaz Mahal was not kept in the showy **cenotaph** that is visible to the public, but rather in a humid crypt beneath the empty tomb.

The Yamuna River (right) was a beautiful site for the Taj Mahal, the resting place of Mumtaz Mahal's tomb (below).

Shah Jahan spared no expense in creating an extravagant tomb in honor of his deceased wife, Mumtaz Mahal. In 1631, he traded four *havelis*, or mansions, for a spacious, gardened area along the left bank of the Yamuna River, in the desert city of Agra.

Shah Jahan sought the most accomplished craftsmen to draw up plans for his queen's tomb, including Ismail Afandi, a prolific dome designer and builder from Turkey; Chiranji Lal, a chief **mosaicist** from Delhi; and Amanat Khan, a master **calligrapher** from Persia.

The emperor then combined ideas from dozens of craft-specific professionals to create an original architectural design that reflects Persian, Central Asian, and Islamic styles.

Shah Jahan recruited 20,000 laborers to build the Taj Mahal. An encampment near the construction site where the workers lived became a bustling city of its own nicknamed "Mumtazabad" after the deceased empress. Work began with crews rerouting the Yamuna so that the river framed the building more beautifully. Laborers then excavated an area about the size of three football fields and added a solid base of gravel to

From the jewel-inlaid white marble of its dome (top left) to the intricate floral motif (top right) and verses from the Koran adorning its walls (bottom), the Taj Mahal is a testament to the expert craftsmanship of its builders.

Even though builders of the Taj Mahal erected a double ceiling within the large marble dome to help bear its massive weight and protect the inside chamber against **monsoon** rains, water leaked through in 1648. Metalworkers repaired the crack with molten silver.

Molten silver (right) was formed into beautiful adornments, while the finest turquoise (below) was sought from distant nations.

keep the structure stable and safe from flooding. They laid a large, square sandstone foundation, or platform. Marble from Makrana, Rajasthan, arrived on carts dragged by teams of elephants and oxen. Masses of laborers used a two-mile (3.2 km) ramp and mule-driven pulleys to guide the marble stones into position to construct the 240-foot-high (73 m) domed tomb.

Next, workers raised two identical buildings on either side of the tomb. The building to the west of the tomb functioned as a **mosque**. The building to the east, known as the *ja-wab*, or "answer," was added only to create architectural balance. At each of the platform's corners, the builders construct-

ed 138-foot-tall (42 m) **minarets**. They purposely built the towers at a slight outward slant so that if one ever toppled, it would not fall on and damage the tomb.

Traditionally, Islamic tombs were not decorated, but Shah Jahan embellished the Taj Mahal in grandiose style. He had rare shells, coral, and pearls collected from the Indian Ocean. He sponsored caravans in search of the best gems, such as jade from China, turquoise from Tibet, and diamonds from Golconda in south India. In all, Shah Jahan purchased 43 different types of precious stones. These shimmering gems adorned the queen's cenotaph in its octagonal burial chamber and decorated the

Although the four elegant minarets that surround the Taj Mahal are not used for religious purposes, each pillar has a letter written on it, which together spell the word ar-rahman ("all merciful")—one of the many Islamic names for Allah, or God.

Visitors to the Taj Mahal might see a number of colorful bird and fish species at or near the site. This includes birds such as large green barbets and koels on the grounds, and great black-headed gulls and river lapwings on the adjacent Yamuna River. Goldfish swim in the marble tank at the center of the site.

front wall of the mausoleum. Elegant black calligraphy and gem-glittered marble screens carved to look like lace accented the inner chamber's beauty.

By the end of 1643, the mausoleum was complete. During the next 10 years, builders constructed the 100-foot-tall (30 m), detached entrance gate, added several secondary buildings, and erected the surrounding wall. Then gardeners turned the grounds into a *charbagh*, a garden of four equal-sized sections said to represent the Islamic Gardens of Paradise, or heaven on Earth. The gardens flourished with scented roses, fruit trees such as date and pomegranate trees, and shade trees such as sycamores, willows, and myrtles. Water channels separated the gardens, symbolizing the rivers of paradise that flowed with water, milk, wine, and honey.

The stunning 42-acre (17 ha) complex took a total of 22 years to complete. Although some historians believe that Shah Jahan built the magnificent Taj Mahal to reflect the high opinion he had of himself, the radiant, graceful building translates as he said he intended: a tribute to the woman he loved.

Lively goldfish (opposite) flit amid the reflection of the Taj Mahal in the central pool of the complex's vibrant gardens (left). The gardens are home to many exotic birds, including barbets (above), while just outside the grounds, the black-headed gull (opposite bottom) can be spotted along the river.

TAJ   MAHAL

Out of respect for the dead, Muslim religious etiquette requires that visitors enter the Taj Mahal's burial chamber in bare feet. A person sits outside by the doorway to ensure that people remove their shoes before entering and to guard the shoes from theft while visitors are inside.

Every day, thousands of visitors from around the world remove their shoes before entering the elaborate doors of the Taj Mahal.

Word of the enormity, expense, and exquisiteness of Shah Jahan's finished project quickly spread worldwide, drawing a growing number of astounded visitors—from jewel merchants to doctors, soldiers to philosophers, princes to presidents. As if the sight of the tomb was not enough, visitors were also drawn by fantastic stories about the emperor who commissioned the tomb.

According to one legend, Shah Jahan cut off the hands of the master builders, blinded the calligraphers, and chopped off the heads of other artists so they could never build another Taj Mahal. Another tale alleged that Shah Jahan planned to build a black marble tomb for himself on the other side of the Yamuna River, but that his son, Aurangzeb, fed up with the frivolousness of his father, refused to build a new monument. When Shah Jahan died in 1666, Aurangzeb stuck the emperor's cenotaph in the Taj Mahal to the right of Mumtaz Mahal, where it rests today.

Unfortunately, about 200 years after the Mogul empire expired in 1707, British **colonizers** treated the majestic grounds as a fanciful picnic area. Married couples rented out the mosques as honeymoon suites. Soon, the gardens became overgrown with

In addition to the Taj Mahal, Shah Jahan also ordered the construction of other beautiful gardens (right), where plants native to India, such as the hibiscus (below), were grown. Today, the influence of modern society can be felt even at his greatest masterpiece, the Taj Mahal.

weeds, trees stopped bearing fruit, waterways dried up, and looters took whatever riches they could pry from the walls and tombs.

At one time, the British planned to tear the Taj Mahal down and sell off the parts. Fortunately, before demolition began, the plan was scrapped because there was not enough demand in England to make it profitable. Later, in the early 1900s, thanks to the forethought of Lord Curzon, a British general who presided over the Indian empire, the Taj Mahal received a substantial overhaul that included repairing chipped mosaics, replacing precious stones, and replanting flowerbeds and trees.

The Taj Mahal, in India's north-central state of Uttar Pradesh, became a protected United Nations Educational, Scientific, and Cultural Organization (UNESCO) World Heritage Site in 1983 because of its historical importance. However, in 2002, the chief minister of Uttar Pradesh secretly approved the Taj Heritage Corridor Project—a plan to begin commercial development on the banks of the Yamuna River within 330 yards (300 m) of the Taj Mahal. The project, not cleared by government agencies, involved the building of multiple shopping complexes and restaurants, as well as an amusement park and

A miniature Taj Mahal stands in Uxbridge, Ontario, built in 1936 by former Toronto (Ontario) mayor Thomas Foster in memory of his late 1920s visit to India. The monument contains burial chambers for his wife, his daughter, and himself.

The crowded streets of India provide a rich tapestry of images, from Western Pepsi advertisements to cows traveling among the many bicyclists.

water park. When the public found out and protested, the plan was aborted, but not before cranes and earth-filling equipment had begun rerouting the Yamuna River. If the work had continued, the Taj Mahal and its gardens might have suffered serious damage due to flooding caused by monsoon rains.

Uttar Pradesh is one of India's poorest, most populous states. More than 2.2 million tourists visit its busy city of Agra every year, finding their way through streets congested with pedestrians, cars, bicycles, **rickshaws**, and, occasionally, a cow or elephant. Exhaust, dust, and smoke from Agra's 200 iron foundries form clouds of smog.

Slums make up housing for most of the city's one and a half million people. Unemployment is extremely high, and along the streets, men, women, and children constantly try to sell their services as guides, shout sales pitches waving postcards and souvenirs, or urge small bears to dance for tips.

Amid this pandemonium and poverty stands the Taj Mahal, an awe-inspiring image of beauty and serenity. Although slightly blemished with marble yellowed from pollution, chips and cracks resulting from age, and original gold **finials** replaced with brass, the Taj Mahal is still widely regarded as the most stunning and unforgettable building in the world.

Near the Taj Mahal—a monument that represents wealth—stand straw huts that embody the poverty of the surrounding nation. More than a third of India's nearly one billion inhabitants live in poverty.

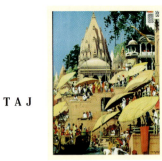

SEEING THE WONDER

Along Agra's streets, at hotel entrances, and in front of the Taj Mahal, visitors may encounter dancing sloth bears, trained by gypsies to beg for money. Although the dancing bear business is illegal, it is a rarely punished crime that removes more than 100 cubs from the wild each year.

Although dancing bears may look cute, tourists are encouraged not to support the business.

Perhaps no other historical monument has drawn tourists to the continent of Asia the way India's Taj Mahal has. The city that is home to this wonder—Agra—is nicknamed "The City of the Taj." Most visitors travel to Agra and the Taj Mahal through Delhi, India's capital. Many of them travel between the cities by plane or by the Shatabdi Express or Taj Express trains. Another popular transportation option is a bus tour; the more expensive bus tours include breakfast, lunch, and tea as well. The region's primary bus

companies also stop at other historic Indian sites along the way.

Visitors are encouraged to enter the Taj Mahal through the site's south gate, as it offers the most spectacular first view of the mausoleum. In 2004, admission to the Taj Mahal cost about $16. The site is open from 7:00 A.M. to 7:00 P.M. every day except Friday. Tourists should be prepared to encounter security guards who may do searches, guides soliciting their services, and swarms of vendors selling souvenirs. Visitors should also be aware that they will need to

The Taj Mahal is approached through a red sandstone gateway that shields the monument from view. The same attention to detail that marks the construction of the Taj Mahal can be seen in the delicate domes (bottom left) and entranceway (bottom right) of the structure.

Just as the Yamuna River reflects the magnificence of the Taj Mahal, the building itself reflects the powerful love of an emperor for his wife.

follow the Muslim custom of removing their shoes before going inside the Taj Mahal to see the cenotaphs.

The desert climate at the Taj Mahal is extreme and tropical. During the summer months of April, May, and June, the heat can be unbearable, hitting 113 °F (45 °C) or more. Monsoons drench Agra from June until September. Most travelers visit during the winter months (November through March). Although the temperatures are more comfortable in the winter, this is also the busiest and most expensive time to go to

India. The months of March, April, September, and October offer fewer crowds and, often, lower hotel rates.

Foreign visitors need to get a passport and visa (documents that allow entrance and specify the purpose and length of the trip) before departing for India. Tourists are encouraged to use an insect repellent containing DEET to protect themselves against mosquitoes that may carry malaria and other diseases. Unpurified drinking water is a frequent cause of illness in India, and tourists are urged to avoid using untreated tap water.

T A J   **M A H A L**

QUICK FACTS

Location: North-central India; the city of Agra in the state of Uttar Pradesh

Age: More than 350 years

Years to complete: 22 (A.D. 1631–53)

Area covered by complex: 42 acres (17 ha)

Height of central dome: 240 feet (73 m)

Weight of central dome: 13,440 tons (12,193 t)

Composition: Masonry (brick and stone) and inlaid marble

Architects: A collection of specialists assembled by Emperor Shah Jahan

Number of workers required for construction: More than 20,000

Geographic setting: Desert

Visitors per year: ~ 2.2 million

Native plant life: Includes hibiscus shrubs, castor plants, and Madagascar periwinkles

Native animal life: Includes Indian peafowl, blue rock pigeons,
Bengal tigers, black buck antelopes, camels, and cobras

GLOSSARY

calligrapher—an artist who specializes in creating beautiful lettering

cenotaph—an empty tomb or monument that honors a dead person who is buried in another place

colonizers—foreigners who settle in an often-distant country their native country has claimed ownership of

finials—needle-shaped decorations that project from the tops of domes

Koran—the holy book of Muslims; it includes revelations that God, or Allah, made to the prophet (holy messenger) Mohammed

lineage—ancestry of the same family, such as the unbroken chain of Mogul emperors who reigned in succession from father to son

minarets—tall towers with balconies; such towers sit at the outer corners of the Taj Mahal's sandstone foundation

Mogul—a term describing the strong, warrior-like emperors who once controlled what is now India

monarchies—systems of government usually ruled by kings or queens whose first-born child is next in line for the throne

monsoon—extreme weather consisting of heavy winds, high humidity, and torrential rains

mosaicist—an artist who specializes in creating designs from small bits of stone, glass, or tile

mosque—a Muslim place of worship

Muslim—a person who follows Islam, the religion in which believers worship one God, Allah, whose prophet is Mohammed

rickshaws—seated carts that are pulled by a motorized or pedaled cycle; they serve much the same purpose as automobile taxis